ACID REFLUX DIET PLAN: Tips on how to quickly avoid and cure GERD

Everlyn Gray

All rights reserved. No part of this publication may be reproduced, distributed, or transmitted in any form or by any means, including photocopying, recording, or other electronic or mechanical methods, without the prior written permission of the publisher, except in the case of brief quotations embodied in critical reviews and certain other noncommercial uses permitted by copyright law.

Copyright © Everlyn Gray, (2022).

Table of contents

Chapter 1

Chapter 2

Chapter 3

Chapter 4

Chapter 5

Introduction

How I completely eliminated GERD and freed myself from years of over-the-counter medications and Acid reflux complications to live a much more comfortable life.
For those who have suffered with it, we know how inconvenient and uncomfortable it can be. You want to get off those medications, but you don't know how to go about it?

This works when everything else fails. This is a step by step book which will guide you on how you can make just a few, simple modifications to your Lifestyle without cutting out all your favourite foods.

In this book, you will find out:
- The real cause of GERD
- How to manage symptoms and become reflux free
- How to build your daily meal plan
- What to do in maintaining your health

Chapter 1

Beginning of gastroesophageal reflux diseases (GERD) Development

The oesophagus, the tube that links your mouth to your stomach, can become inflamed and cause acid reflux when the contents of your stomach ascend up it.
Most people occasionally have minor reflux. When the reflux is mild, there is often little chance of problems.

Contrarily, persistent acid reflux can be a symptom of gastroesophageal reflux disease (GERD).
Acid reflux that is mild or sporadic normally poses little danger. Although it could produce

brief discomfort, there are no significant health hazards.

The lower esophageal sphincter (LES) which is the typical anatomic valve between the oesophagus and stomach, allows food and liquids to flow through into your stomach when you usually swallow. For food and fluids to enter the stomach, the LES relaxes. To reduce food and liquid reflux from the stomach into the oesophagus, the normal LES then tightens once again.

However, sometimes the LES relaxes improperly, allowing stomach contents to reflux back into the oesophagus. It sometimes occurs to everyone. The majority of these episodes take place soon after meals, are brief, and are symptomless. In most cases, reflux shouldn't happen when you're asleep.

Your esophageal sphincter relaxes between swallows when you have GERD, enabling stomach acid to enter your oesophagus.

Hydrochloric acid is produced in your stomach during the digestive process. Your oesophagus does not generate mucus, although the lining of your stomach does, protecting it from erosion. The lining of your oesophagus becomes irritated by digesting acid from your stomach when reflux happens. This acid rests at the bottom of your oesophagus and regulates what goes in and out of it.

GERD, if left untreated can result in serious complications which increases the risk of esophageal injury such as:

Esophagitis
Esophagitis, which is characterised by esophageal inflammation, can result from untreated GERD. Esophagitis can cause esophageal bleeding, ulcers, and permanent scarring. The entire oesophagus may eventually become narrowed as a result of this scarring, making swallowing exceedingly challenging.

stomach ulcers

One of the main causes of ulcers, which are uncomfortable open sores or lesions that develop in the lining of the oesophagus, is untreated GERD. Esophageal ulcers are frequent among GERD sufferers because their oesophagus is constantly exposed to stomach acid.

Oesophagus with Barrett's
The lining of your oesophagus's cells may also alter as a result of stomach acid. Barrett's oesophagus is the name given to this alteration. Although it is not particularly prevalent, Barrett's oesophagus can raise the risk of esophageal cancer. Approximately 5–10% of GERD sufferers will never develop Barrett's oesophagus.

The GERD Stages
When stomach contents leak into the oesophagus, it is known as gastroesophageal reflux disease (GERD) (reflux). Even though GERD is widespread, the problem is chronic, therefore it's crucial to understand what stage

you have if you want to get the right care. The frequency and intensity of your symptoms determine the stage of GERD.

First stage: Mild GERD
Mild symptoms appear in patients once or twice each month. Lifestyle modifications and over-the-counter acid suppressants are the mainstays of treatment.

Second stage: Moderate GERD
Patients have more frequent symptoms that call for daily doses of acid-suppressing prescription drugs. The everyday activities of the patient are impacted by untreated GERD symptoms, which are linked to esophageal inflammation.

Third stage: Severe GERD
Patients with severe GERD struggle to manage their symptoms with prescribed drugs. Their standard of living is far lower. The likelihood of patients having erosive esophageal inflammation is higher. It is very advised to get a full examination from a GERD specialist. GERD is

cured with an effective anti-reflux technique that strengthens the lower esophageal sphincter and enhances patient quality of life.

Fourth stage: Esophageal cancer or reflux-induced precancerous tumours

This is the outcome of severe reflux that has gone untreated for several years. 10% of GERD sufferers develop to stage 4 of the condition. They get Barrett's oesophagus, a precancerous disease. If left untreated, Barrett's oesophagus might develop into cancer. The goal of various Barrett's oesophagus therapy approaches is to stop the condition from developing into cancer. It is very advised to have close monitoring and care by a reflux specialist.

Most GERD sufferers are at stage 1, which is characterised by mild regurgitation and/or heartburn. Mild esophageal irritation is frequently caused by this stage of GERD.

GERD is often easily treatable, but to do so, you must be knowledgeable about its causes and symptoms.

Chapter 2

Gerd and Heartburn

Heartburn is typically described as a searing pain behind the breast bone in the middle of the chest. The throat may feel its upward radiation. The primary cause of heartburn is frequent esophageal acid reflux.

The burning feeling is brought on by the fact that the lining of the oesophagus is significantly more sensitive to acid than the stomach. Persistent heartburn in those with gastroesophageal reflux disease (GERD) can be uncomfortable, interfere with everyday activities, and cause nighttime awakenings.

A sign is a heartburn. Over 44% of adult Americans are thought to have heartburn at least once each month, making it a relatively common condition. The acid that causes heartburn, however, has the potential to harm the lining of the oesophagus if it happens frequently. It may lead to ulceration, which could result in pain or even bleeding.

Acid reflux that is chronic and recurrent can also produce stricture, which is the narrowing of the oesophagus brought on by acid and results in the production of scar tissue. Food is challenging for those who have strictures to swallow.

Patients with or without erosive GERD cannot be distinguished based on the severity, frequency, or intensity of their symptoms. However, indigestion happens a lot more often than once every week, increases in severity, or happens at night and awakens a person

The most frequently reported GERD symptom is chronic heartburn. Another typical symptom is acid reflux (refluxed acid into the mouth), which is occasionally accompanied by a sour or bitter taste.

Heartburn is just one of many symptoms linked to GERD. These may include:

Belching

trouble swallowing
waterbrash (sudden excess of saliva).
Laryngitis with a persistent sore throat
prolonged coughing
clearing of the throat
associated oral problems such as gum irritation and tooth enamel erosion
early morning hoarseness
a foul taste or poor breath
Chronic wheeze from asthma and noncardiac chest pain (it may feel like angina)

In the absence of the symptoms listed above, dysphagia—the sensation that food is stuck in the oesophagus—is an unusual and serious sign that requires immediate medical attention.

Heartburn Home Remedies
Antacids, which are over-the-counter drugs that reduce stomach acid, are frequently used by people who have heartburn.
However, taking them for a long period of time can either cause constipation or have a laxative

effect. Some people have had allergic reactions. Antacids might also increase the risk of developing sensitivities to certain foods.

But, certain meals may also provide symptom alleviation. Try the following, perhaps:

Milk
Does milk aid with heartburn relief? According to Gupta, milk is frequently believed to cure heartburn. "But you must bear in mind that there are several types of milk, including whole milk with all the fat, 2% fat, and skim or nonfat milk. Milk fat might make acid reflux symptoms worse. Nonfat milk, however, can temporarily obstruct the stomach lining from the stomach's acidic contents and offer quick relief from heartburn symptoms." The same calming effects are present in low-fat yoghurts, which also contain plenty of probiotics (good bacteria that enhance digestion).

Ginger
Due to its therapeutic qualities, ginger is one of the greatest foods to help with digestion. Its natural alkalinity and anti-inflammatory properties reduce digestive system inflammation. If you start to have heartburn, try drinking some ginger tea.

ACV, apple cider
Even though there isn't enough evidence to support it, many individuals firmly believe that consuming apple cider vinegar relieves acid reflux. However, because it contains a strong acid that might irritate the oesophagus, you shouldn't ever consume it when fully concentrated. Instead, mix a little bit with warm water and consume it together with meals.

lemon juice
Lemon juice is generally considered very acidic, but a small amount of lemon juice mixed with warm water and honey has an alkalizing effect

that neutralises stomach acid. Also, honey has natural antioxidants, which protect the health of cells.

Chapter 3

High Risk Factors of Developing GERD

GERD may be brought on by a variety of factors. Your GERD may occasionally have a complex underlying cause that involves several factors.

Lower Esophageal Sphincter (LES) relaxation is the most common cause of acid reflux in sufferers. The LES controls the closure and opening of the lower end of the oesophagus and functions as a pressure barrier to the contents of the stomach. The LES will not fully close after food enters your stomach if it is weak or loses tone. The oesophagus may then become flooded with stomach acid.

Since the lining of the oesophagus differs from that of the stomach and is less resilient to acid exposure, it is more prone to injury. The symptoms and potential harm to the oesophagus are brought on by this acid reflux into it.

Certain foods and drinks, drugs, and other substances can weaken the LES and impair its function, though sometimes this dysfunction is structural.

Obesity: Being obese puts more pressure on your abdomen, which aggravates GERD symptoms.

Though the precise relationship between GERD and obesity is not fully understood, being obese is thought to be both a risk factor and a potential cause of GERD.

Medication: Several medications may influence a person's risk of developing GERD and worsening symptoms.

Aspirin, Motrin or Advil (ibuprofen), and Aleve (naproxen) are examples of nonsteroidal anti-inflammatory drugs (NSAIDs), and gastrointestinal side effects are frequent when taking them. These drugs are frequently linked to the development of peptic ulcers, and they may exacerbate heartburn and esophageal irritation by weakening or relaxing the LES.

These drugs may exacerbate GERD symptoms in those who already have them, while prolonged NSAID use may increase the risk of GERD in those without the condition.
The symptoms of GERD may also be brought on by or made worse by some prescription drugs

Scleroderma: An autoimmune condition called scleroderma affects the body's connective tissues, including the oesophagus. In the case of GERD, it can lead to esophageal dysfunction and makes the afflicted regions hard or fibrous.

Gastroparesis: Delayed stomach emptying is a symptom that is frequently observed in persons with type 1 diabetes. The risk of having GERD increases when the stomach does not empty completely and does not digest the acid. This might lead to excess pressure in the stomach.

COPD: Your chance of having GERD may rise if you have COPD or chronic obstructive pulmonary disease. Additionally, having GERD exacerbates the symptoms of COPD.

Smoking: Smoking and exposure to secondhand smoke are both known to increase the chance of getting GERD.
Smoking may cause heartburn in a variety of ways, including reducing salivation, slowing down stomach emptying, and increasing stomach acid production. Quitting smoking is likely one of the greatest things you can do to alleviate your symptoms or reduce your chance of first acquiring reflux.

Hiatal Hernia: A hiatal hernia happens when the muscle wall that separates the stomach from the chest—the diaphragm—is breached by the upper portion of your stomach. This reduces the reflux-causing pressure on the LES. Any age may develop a hiatal hernia, and many otherwise healthy adults over 50 have a tiny one.

Impaired Stomach Function: People with GERD may have the abnormal nerve or muscle activity in the stomach, which slows down the digestion of food and stomach acid. This delays the stomach's ability to empty its contents, increasing the internal pressure and raising the risk of acid reflux.

Motility Disorders: During normal digestion, rhythmic contractions known as peristalsis move food through the digestive tract. These contractions are abnormal if you have a digestive motility disorder. A problem with the muscle itself or a problem with the nerves or hormones that regulate the muscle's contractions can both be the cause of this abnormality.

Pregnancy: The LES is relaxed during pregnancy due to an increase in the hormones estrogen and progesterone, as well as the added pressure from your growing belly. Because of this, heartburn in pregnant women is fairly common and can result in GERD.

Foods: If you seldom get heartburn, eating is often not a trigger for an episode. But if you have it often, you may find that certain meals or just eating too much of anything appears to set it off. Some options increase acid production while others cause the LES to relax.

Examples of foods that can unwind the LES include the following:

greasy, fried foods

fattening meats

Margarine and butter

Mayonnaise

whipped sauces

dressings for salads

dairy goods made with whole milk

Chocolate

Peppermint

Liquids that include caffeine such as:
soft drinks
coffee
tea
and cocoa

Foods That Stimulate Acid Production: If your stomach creates too much acid, it may back up into your oesophagus, causing heartburn.

The following foods may aggravate heartburn and accelerate the formation of acid:

Caffeinated drinks

Caffeinated drinks

Alcohol

hot foods

roasted pepper

Juices and citrus fruits, such as orange and grapefruit

tomato nectar

Salt: Research has shown that a diet heavy in salt may contribute to GERD by causing acid reflux. An extremely salty diet doesn't seem to worsen acid reflux in healthy individuals, either. More research is required, however salt may at the very least be a heartburn trigger for certain individuals. The only way to be certain is to try reducing your salt consumption and observe any effects.

Chapter 4

Changes to Diet- Best foods for a refluxer

Diet is the primary line of treatment for GERD patients and has a vital role in managing acid reflux symptoms.

It's not necessary to give up all of your favourite meals to eat healthfully if you have GERD. It is frequently sufficient to change your diet just a little bit.

Fibre-rich foods

Fibrous meals help you feel full, which lowers your risk of overeating, which can worsen heartburn. So, fill up on these foods' beneficial fibre:

Oatmeal, couscous, and brown rice are examples of whole grains.

Sweet potatoes, carrots, and beets are examples of root vegetables.

green foods including green beans, broccoli, and asparagus.

Astringent foods
Foods are pH-scale-dependent in some way. Low-pH foods are acidic and more prone to cause reflux than those with a higher pH. Higher pH values are alkaline and can help counteract very acidic stomach contents. Alkaline meals consist of:

Bananas

Melons

Cauliflower

Fennel

Nuts

Watery dishes
Consuming foods high in water can weaken and dilute stomach acid. Select foods like:

Celery

Cucumber

Lettuce

Watermelon

soups made with broth

flavoured tea

Veggies and fruits

Fruits: Choose from a selection of non-citrus fruits, such as bananas, melons, apples, and pears among others, while probably avoiding citrus fruits and juices, such as oranges and lemons.

Vegetables: Choose from the extensive selection of veggies. Avoid or cut back on fatty sauces and garnishes, as well as other irritants like tomatoes and onions.

Healthy proteins
Eggs: These contain a lot of protein. The higher-fat yolks, which are more prone to result in symptoms, should be avoided if eggs are an issue for you; instead, stick to the whites.

fatty meat: Low pressure in the lower esophageal sphincter (LES) and delayed stomach emptying from high-fat meals and fried foods increase the risk of reflux. Pick lean meats that have been baked, broiled, poached, or grilled.

Complex Carbohydrates

Whole grain bread, couscous, rice, and oatmeal. These are all excellent sources of beneficial complex carbohydrates. Fibre is added to your diet through whole grains and brown rice.

Optimal Fats

High in calories yet essential to your diet, fat is a type of nutrient. Fats are not created equally. Avoid or limit your consumption of trans fats, which are often found in meat and dairy products (in processed foods, kinds of margarine, and shortenings). Replace them with unsaturated fats from vegetables or seafood in moderation. Here are a few instances:

Monounsaturated fatty acids. Examples include avocados, peanuts, and peanut butter, various nuts and seeds, and oils including olive, sesame, canola, and sunflower.

Polyunsaturated fatty acids. Examples include oils such as safflower soybean, maize, flaxseed, and walnut oils, as well as soybeans and tofu, as well as fatty fish like salmon and trout, are some examples.

Chapter 5

Lifestyle Modification and Self care- Reflux free

Some GERD symptoms can be reduced by making lifestyle changes. The most effective GERD treatments at this stage generally concentrate on modifying one's lifestyle. A few lifestyle risk factors are linked to GERD development. These are elements that you can alter or manage.

Coming up with the appropriate diet and lifestyle changes involves discovering what works best for you. Not all triggers and treatments will affect all people in the same way. Bear in mind that when you eat may be just as important as what you eat. A particular food that causes reflux when eaten 3–4 hours before bedtime may be harmless earlier in the day

A GERD-friendly eating plan, which is essentially a high-protein diet that avoids certain foods, is superior to medication because it can prevent or stop reflux when combined with a few other lifestyle changes.

Let's first focus on the elements of a high-protein diet and then move on to the necessary lifestyle changes that will help you enjoy eating again, reflux-free.

Designing a high- protein diet that works for You

The goal of a GERD-friendly high protein diet is to reduce your acid reflux symptoms, and that type of diet has several attributes:

Low-fat content – Less fat requires less bile and acid for digestion and faster digestion time.

High-protein content – More protein per ounce, more health benefits.

Correct portion size – We think a 3.5 – 4.0 ounce is ideal for high-protein meats with an additional ounce or two for fish based on the fat content. Total daily consumption should be around 6.0 ounces.

High protein diet that is low in overall fat and saturated fat

There are a lot of foods that contain protein such as beef, chicken, and fish. However, it is important to differentiate between low-fat and high-fat selections.

"If you want to follow a high-protein diet, choose your protein wisely. Good choices include soy protein, beans, nuts, fish, skinless poultry, lean beef, pork, and low-fat dairy products. Avoid processed meats."

For example, red meats are packed with protein, vitamin B-12, and iron. Some cuts are much leaner in fat than others as noted in the lists below:

Sirloin tip steak – 4 oz. – 7 g fat / 3 g Sat fat / 23 g protein

Eye of round steak – 4 oz. – 10 g fat / 4 g Sat fat / 23 g protein

Top sirloin steak – 4 oz. – 12 g fat / 5 g Sat fat / 23 g protein

New York strip steak – 4 oz.- 17 g fat / 7 g Sat fat / 23 g protein

Fillet mignon – 4 oz. – 20 g fat / 8 g Sat fat / 29 g protein

Fish have similar, but improved nutritional profiles. However, there is still a significant difference between high-fat and low-fat fish. As you can see from the list below, the fish selection is important as well:

Cod (broiled) – 6 oz. – 2 g fat / 0 g Sat fat / 38 g protein

Rainbow trout (broiled) – 6 oz. – 8 g fat / 2 g Sat fat / 44 g protein

Swordfish (broiled) – 6 oz. – 8 g fat / 2 g Sat fat / 42 g protein

Atlantic salmon (baked) – 6 oz. – 14 g fat / 2 g Sat fat / 44 g protein

These nutritional profiles highlight that selection from within different food groups is critical to how much fat and protein we consume, along with the potential for acid reflux symptoms. Less fat means faster digestion with less acid and fewer symptoms.

You still need fats and carbohydrates in your diet. You need balance in your high protein diet, and some fats and carbohydrates are an important part of a healthy diet.

Carbohydrates are important since they provide much of your body's short-term energy, so we don't want to skimp here. Proteins are for energy too, but it takes longer to break them down than carbohydrates. Fats are also critical to your body since they improve vitamin absorption, which is necessary for your immune system. But as we know, too much fat can also cause severe health issues.

There is a wide range in the number of grams of carbohydrates, fats, and proteins that you can consume daily. For an adult targeting a calorie intake of 1,990 calories, a goal might be something like this:

Carbohydrates – 236 g

Proteins – 95 g

Fats – 63 g

Since that is a target, and our diet changes day to day, consider a daily range such as those noted below:

Carbohydrates – 200 g to 300 g

Proteins – 50 g to 170 g

Fats – 45 g to 75 g

Lifestyle Changes to Compliment Your High Protein

Eating more protein is a great start, but you are not done. We recommend several lifestyle changes that should be made as part of a comprehensive program to reduce GERD symptoms.

Following these patterns often helps to reduce the symptoms of GERD:

Eating patterns:
Eat small, frequent meals rather than large ones.

Avoid eating three hours before night and avoid eating just before bed.

Consider consuming smaller, more frequent meals.

To try to avoid milk, try drinking a lot of water.

Avoid foods and drinks including chocolate, wine, coffee, citrus, spicy meals, fatty foods, and tomato-based goods since they may exacerbate your symptoms.

Quit smoking since it increases your chance of getting GERD.

Gum chewing increases saliva production and lowers the amount of acid in the oesophagus (but not spearmint or peppermint, which can relax the LES).

Exercise habits: It's important to keep in mind that obesity is both a cause and a risk factor for GERD. You are more likely to get GERD if you are overweight, especially around your abdominal region. To some extent, GERD may be controlled by making an effort to maintain a healthy weight.
Running, powerlifting, jumping rope, and other high-impact workouts may significantly worsen GERD symptoms.

For those who suffer from acid reflux, more moderate and low-impact exercises are advised. Exercises like:
light jogging

yoga

stationary cycling

and swimming with light weights are all recommended.

Mostly, this can assist you in losing weight, which will lessen GERD and acid reflux symptoms.

Sleeping habits: There are several reasons why GERD is often worse at night after going to bed. Gravity no longer works to keep stomach acid down while one is laying down, which makes reflux more likely. During sleep, swallowing is reduced, which lessens a significant force that pulls stomach acid downhill. Although saliva may help neutralize stomach acid, less saliva is produced in the latter phases of sleep.

These effects may combine to make it easier for stomach acid to flow into the oesophagus and to stay there for longer, possibly leading to more severe GERD symptoms, including those that might interfere with sleep.

The following sleeping postures can lessen your risk of reflux:
Sleeping with your head raised or raising the bed's head by six inches when lying on your left side

Manufactured by Amazon.ca
Bolton, ON